MIND OF A HUSTLER

GREG WASHINGTON
with
MALIKA WASHINGTON

MIND OF A HUSTLER

For Ken Carlos

FINAL DISPOSITION   SC-6

IN THE SUPERIOR COURT OF FULTON COUNTY

STATE OF GEORGIA

VS.

Washington, Gregory

FINAL DISPOSITION

CRIMINAL ACTION NO. 02SC02245

OFFENSE(S) 16-13-31 Trafficking In Cocaine
possession of fircarm by
Convicted felon 16-11-131
Sept - Oct _____ TERM, 2002

☐ PLEA:	☑ JURY	☐ VERDICT:	☐ OTHER DISPOSITION

☐ NEGOTIATED
☐ GUILTY ON COUNT(S) _____
☐ NOLO CONTENDERE ON
COUNT(S) _____
☐ TO LESSER INCLUDED
OFFENSE(S) _____
ON COUNT(S) _____

☐ JURY
☐ NON-JURY

☑ GUILTY ON
COUNT(S) 1
☐ NOT GUILTY ON
COUNT(S) _____
☐ GUILTY OF INCLUDED
OFFENSE(S) OF _____
ON COUNT(S) _____

☐ NOLLE PROSEQUI ORDER ON
COUNT(S) _____
☑ DEAD DOCKET ORDER ON
COUNT(S) 2
(SEE SEPARATE ORDER)

☑ DEFENDANT WAS ADVISED OF HIS/HER RIGHT TO HAVE THIS SENTENCE REVIEWED BY THE SUPERIOR COURT'S SENTENCE REVIEW PANEL.

☑ FELONY SENTENCE   ☐ MISDEMEANOR SENTENCE

WHEREAS, the above-named defendant has been found guilty of the above-stated offense, WHEREUPON, it is ordered and adjudged by the Court that: The said defendant is hereby sentenced to confinement for a period of _____ Twenty (20)years to serve _____

in the State Penal System or such other institution as the Commissioner of the State Department of Corrections or Court may direct, to be computed as provided by law. HOWEVER, it is further ordered by the Court

☐ 1) THAT the above sentence may be served on probation

☐ 2) THAT upon service of _____ the above sentence, the remainder of _____ may be served on probation PROVIDED that the said defendant complies with the following general and other conditions herein imposed by the Court as a part of this sentence.

☐ 3) THAT the above sentence be suspended.

☐ GENERAL CONDITIONS OF PROBATION

The defendant, having been granted the privilege of serving all or part of the above-stated sentence on probation, hereby is sentenced to the following general conditions of probation:

☐ 1) Do not violate the criminal laws of any governmental unit.
☐ 2) Avoid injurious and vicious habits - especially alcoholic intoxication and narcotics and other dangerous drugs unless prescribed lawfully.
☐ 3) Avoid persons or places of disreputable or harmful character.
☐ 4) Report to the Probation-Parole Supervisor as directed and permit such Supervisor to visit him (her) at home or elsewhere.
☐ 5) Work faithfully at suitable employment insofar as may be possible.
☐ 6) Do not change his (her) place of abode, move outside the jurisdiction of the Court, or leave the State for any period of time without prior permission of the Probation Supervisor.
☐ 7) Support his (her) legal dependants to the best of his (her) ability.
☐ 8) Probationer shall, from time to time upon oral or written request by any Probation Officer, produce a breath, urine, and/or blood specimen for analysis for the possible presence of a substance prohibited or controlled by any law of the State of Georgia or of the United States.

☐ OTHER CONDITIONS OF PROBATION

IT IS FURTHER ORDERED that the defendant pay a fine in the amount of $ _____ plus $50 or 10%, whichever is less pursuant to O.C.G.A. 15-21-70 plus 10% of the original fine pursuant to O.C.G.A. 15-21-90 and pay restitution in the amount of $ _____ Probation Fee $ _____ and Court Costs $ _____

☐ Plus 50% of Original Fine _____ Pursuant to OCGA 15-21-100.

IT IS THE FURTHER ORDER of the Court, and the defendant is hereby advised that the Court may, at any time, revoke any conditions of this probation and/or discharge the defendant from probation. The probationer shall be subject to arrest for violation of any condition of probation herein granted. If such probation is revoked, the Court may order the execution of the sentence which was originally imposed or any portion thereof in the manner provided by law after deducting therefrom the amount of time the defendant has served on probation.

The defendant was represented by the Honorable Daniel Gavrin _____ Attorney at Law (Employment) (Appointment)

So ordered this 31st day of October 2002 _____

Court Reporter: Evelyn Parker

Judge, Fulton Superior Court

CERTIFICATE OF SERVICE

This is to certify that a true and correct copy of this Sentence of Probation has been delivered in person to the defendant and he/she instructed regarding the conditions as set forth above.

This _____ day of _____

_____
Probation Officer

Copy received and instructions regarding conditions acknowledge.

This _____ day of _____

_____
Probationer
16b-31-1287

White - Clerk   Canary - Defendant   Pink - Probation Office   Goldenrod - Sheriff

BOOK _____ PAGE _____
0050 - 194

FOREWORD

Having known Greg Washington for more than a dozen years and observing him as he has served in multiple leadership roles, I am not surprised by the success he is now experiencing as he works to prepare men currently incarcerated for reentry and reintegration. Nor am I surprised by the fact that he is a strong husband, leads a great family, and serves his community with a servant's heart.

Greg's story is one that represents the highs and lows of life and a little bit of everything in between. It is a story that inspires and challenges, motivates and encourages, and, ultimately, invites the reader to consider their own life and how their story can be used to impact others in positive ways. Greg's honesty about his own bad choices and the consequences associated with those choices is refreshing, and his message of overcoming those consequences gives everyone hope that they too can rise above any past failures and be successful as they move forward.

It is his faith that stands out most powerfully as Greg shares. He acknowledges that his current place in life is directly related to his relationship and obedience to God Almighty, and it's that part of Greg's story that will live far beyond the writing of a book or his current role in life.

Knowing Greg Washington is an honor, and I highly recommend his story as one that should be read by all.

BRUCE DEEL
Founder/CEO of the City of Refuge Atlanta

Greg Washington is the Director of Family Reunification and
Reentry at City of Refuge in Atlanta, Georgia.
He is married to Malika Washington, and they have five children.

This is a work of creative nonfiction.
The events are portrayed to the best of Greg Washington's memory.
While all the stories in this book are true,
some names and identifying details have been changed
to protect the privacy of the people involved.

Library of Congress Control Number: 2020900585

ISBN 978-0-578-60007-9—Paperback

Hustle
verb
hust-le
hustled; hustling

transitive verb
1 a: to crowd or push roughly; JOSTLE, SHOVE
   had been *hustled* into a jail cell with other protesters
  b: to convey forcibly or hurriedly
     "...grabbed him by the arm and *hustled* him out the door..."
     —*John Dos Passos*
  c: to urge forward precipitately *hustling* tourists from one
     museum to the next

2 a: to obtain by energetic activity, usually used with *up*
     - *hustle* up new customers
     - try to *hustle* up some tickets to tonight's game
     - *hustling* up some grub
  b: to sell something or to obtain something from (someone) by
     energetic and especially **underhanded activity: SWINDLE**
     - ***hustling the suckers***
     - **an elaborate scam to** *hustle* **the elderly**
  c: to sell or promote energetically and aggressively
     hustling a new product
  d: to lure less skillful players into competing against oneself at
     (a gambling game) *hustle* pool

intransitive verb
1 : SHOVE, PRESS
2 : HASTEN, HURRY, you'd better *hustle* if you want to catch
   the bus
3 a : to make a strenuous effort to obtain especially money or
     business
     "Our quartet was out *hustling*...and we knew we stood good
     to take in a lot of change before the night was over."
     —*Louis Armstrong*
  b : to obtain money by fraud or deception
  c : to engage in prostitution
4 : to play a game or sport in an alert aggressive manner
     "She's not the most talented player on the team, but she
     always *hustles*."

GREG TWENTY YEARS AGO

On October 31, 2002, Greg Washington was sentenced to twenty years in the Georgia Department of Corrections for trafficking cocaine. He had no idea that his life would be drastically changed, for the better, as a result of being incarcerated.

CHAPTER ONE

THE FOUNDATION

I grew up in the early seventies in the H-Town, also known as Houston, Texas. The seventies offered my family, and many other Americans, a sense of hope. The Vietnam War that had nearly crippled the US finally came to an end. After twelve long months of fighting for his country, my father returned home. Dad didn't talk much about his time in combat. I'm sure he suffered some scars, lost some buddies, and experienced one trauma too many, but those details of his life remained a mystery. Many began to take a more personal approach to life; they were less impressed with wars and politics and focused more on developing a sense of identity and expressing themselves.

Bellbottoms, platform shoes, afros, and slangs like *"Catch you on the flip side"* captivated the culture. As a child, I spent a lot of time with my mother's brothers. They took me to just about every main attraction in Houston. Uncle Warren bought season passes for AstroWorld every year. He would always invite me. I can still remember standing in line, for what seemed like forever, to ride the Texas Cyclone.

For an extra thrill, I made sure to sit in the last cart on the coaster. It would nearly come off of the tracks on every drop. No matter if they were rich or poor, black, white, or Hispanic, almost every Texan parent in the seventies made sure their children had at least one pair of cowboy boots. There was no way you could be from Texas and not dress the part. My mother bought me the cleanest pair of cream, ostrich-skin cowboy boots, with the hat and belt to match. I'd try to wear those same three pieces with every outfit for Texan Day at school on Wednesdays and to the Texas Rodeo that came to town every year. I got mad when I couldn't fit the boots anymore.

My Uncle Warren took me to my first Houston Rockets game. The smell of buttery popcorn and cheers from fans rooting for the Houston Rockets always cause me to reminisce about the Summit. My childhood consisted of fond memories. But, as I take a closer look at the seventies, I'm forced to see where I had my first encounters with hustling.

My mother's oldest brother worked for the City of Houston, for over a decade. He had the most beautiful house I've ever seen. I would love to visit with his family on the weekends. Plus, he was far from cheap. He would always make sure I had the latest and greatest of everything. I looked up to Uncle. Much to my surprise, the seemingly comfortable life he lived didn't only come from working for the City; he also sold marijuana on the side for twenty-three years. As a child, I didn't know what he did to make extra money, but I had a gut feeling that it was more than punching a time clock at the office.

"Mary Jane" was considered nothing more than a harmless recreational drug back then. Getting high was second nature. Not too many saw anything wrong with it. I'm sure Uncle thought selling a little weed wouldn't hurt anyone. I suppose he thought he was making a living for his family. No matter if they're a beginner or have a PhD in street pharmacology, all hustlers have a purpose for hustling.

After years of instability and tumultuousness, my mother and father went their separate ways. I was six years old at the time. Without much of a discussion, my parents decided that I would live with my mother. Unlike many young boys after their parents' separation, I wasn't left without a positive male influence. Several months after my parents' breakup, Mom met Dan. Aside from my uncles, Dan was the first man to attend my baseball and Pop Warner games.

He took Mom and me on our first boating trip that his supervisor invited him to. We would go to the beach and other outings. Dan had a great work ethic; he worked hard every day. He was a provider; he cared for his family. I admired that about him. But, like my uncle, Dan had a side hustle. Uncle would front Dan weed to sell. Dan sold it in our community. Unfortunately, Dan and Mom got into a disagreement that crushed their relationship. After four years of experiencing a stable two-parent home, he split. Mom and I were alone again.

I was an only child, which made it a little easier for Mom to take care of me. She always worked to make sure I had all of my needs, and most of my wants, met. Mom and I moved to a low-income housing community when I was around ten years old. A new idea settled into my mind around that time. I saw how hard she worked. I suppose it was my instinct—the same instinct most little boys have—to want to help my mother. I would ask our maintenance man if I could work with him during the summers. He put me on staff; I helped him clean up apartments and take out the trash. I earned about ninety dollars over the summer. I used that money to take care of some of my "wants" that Mom wasn't able to.

Even though Mom and Dad weren't always on the best of terms, she was cool with me spending time with him. Of course, there were aspects of life and manhood that she just wasn't equipped to teach me. When I turned thirteen, I moved to Inglewood, California, with my father. Living in Cali was very much like a scene out of *Menace II Society*, before the

Hughes brothers came up with the story. We lived on 102nd Street and Doty, a Raymond Avenue Crip neighborhood, but I went to Monroe Junior High, which was in the Crenshaw Mafia Blood community.

The school administrators would let the 102nd students out of school early, hoping to get us past the daily beatdowns from the Bloods. Although I wasn't in a gang, the fact that I lived in a Crip community automatically made me a target. The fact that I was best friends with Chucky, whose big brother was Mad Dog, a 97 Murder Street Crip, made matters worse. Almost every Crenshaw Mafia Blood knew Chucky was Mad Dog's brother. Mad Dog was as crazy as they came. A creased pair of pants, tennis shoes, a buttoned-down blue flannel, sunglasses, and a blue rag hanging from his pocket was his everyday wear. He would stand on top of the roof of our apartment building shooting at Bloods as they drove by. Each day the school bell rang for the 102nd Street walkers, Chucky and I would run out the building as if our lives depended on it, which they did. We didn't stop until we made it home.

The conditions of the infamous gangs that we know of were never intended to be what they've become—a blatant disregard for people and life itself. Black and Latino gangs in California originally formed as clubs, as a form of protection against racism that ensued in the sixties. Gangs in LA became most violent against one another, as we see so often today. The majority of gangs I knew of were made up of teenage boys and young men in their early twenties who had no sense of identity. Not knowing who we are is dangerous; we'll be more likely to believe the lies Satan (and people) declares over our lives. We'll become more concerned about the short-lived identities others give us, rather than the lasting uniqueness God gives us. Dependency on others for our validation is sure to follow.

Most of the gang members I knew were fatherless or had a father who was present, but not there. They were products of unfortunate circumstances that weren't their fault. Most of them never heard, *"Good job, son."* Their fathers may not have attended any of their Pee-Wee games or award ceremonies. They longed for acceptance, mostly because their first line of defense—their families—failed to provide them with the affirmation they needed as children.

"Family" becomes the homies and "Big Homie" replaces "Dad." They wanted to be a part of something, anything, that would give them a sense of value—even if it meant selling drugs, killing, robbing, womanizing, and putting their families in danger. And as grown men, they are somehow still little boys that don't understand their worth.

Dad was the "rent man" for one of the housing communities. He worked for the owner of the property and collected rent from all of the tenants, on the first of the month. Like Uncle and Dan, Dad also had a side hustle. Dad was a "rent man" by day and a pusher-man by night; he sold PCP and marijuana. I wasn't a teenager for a full year and I already experienced three relevant men in my life who sold drugs. They were creating a very shaky foundation for me. Without me knowing it, Dad, Uncle, and Dan deposited something into my life. I liked the idea of being able to make my own money—and fast.

I landed my second job selling *Daily Breeze* newspapers, at Hollywood Park. *"Get ya daily Breeze, we got your pick six, daily double exacters, we have Mason, Single, and Lucky Louise,"* was my sales pitch. I worked in the Clubhouse, where all of the celebrities and big spenders visited. Arnold Schwarzenegger, the late John Ritter, and the late Vic Tayback were a few of the passersby. On a good day, I made about a hundred twenty-six dollars, which wasn't bad for a thirteen-year-old in those days.

I worked the racetrack gig as a summer hustle. When it got cold, I pumped gas at one of the local gas stations for money, until another business venture presented itself. A new hustle was shortly on the horizon. A few of the community kids and I loaded up in a fifteen-passenger van on weekends with our new "supervisor," Mr. Joe. Joe would stop by Mayfield Grocery stores and buy all of the candy and chocolate bars he could carry and afford. We'd drive out to the well-off communities to sell everything Joe purchased at a much higher price. With a fake spiel of being in a youth organization, raising money for a trip to Camp Big Bear, I eagerly went door-to-door selling Borden Thin Mints.

I soon realized that making money wasn't that hard. Instant gratification infiltrated my young mind. I thought, *I could sell something and get paid on the spot?* There was no waiting for a weekly paycheck. Instant gratification rules out the need to wait; it forces us to develop an "I want mine now" mindset, which is dangerous. Yes, we live in a microwave society, where everyone wants everything in a heartbeat. Unbeknownst to us, we're developing impulsive traits that strip us of our ability to maintain self-control.

Sadly, the mindset that I was adopting was the same that most young people in poor communities assume—whether it was selling candy door-to-door or selling bottles of water and candied apples on the corner. Unfortunately, children who have the most trouble delaying gratification have higher rates of incarceration as adults *(Psychology Today, 2012)*. There is nothing wrong, per se, with selling candy and water for extra money. However, if young people's desire to earn money is not knitted together with morals, it'll be easy for those innocent acts to become dark—leading to issues in our communities. My underdeveloped and distorted "salesman" mentality, which most hustlers begin with, was a surefire way to start creating a mind of a hustler.

I was good at working with our neighborhood's maintenance man, I was good at selling papers, I was good at selling candy; inevitably selling crack-cocaine would be a cakewalk. Before I knew it, the money I made wasn't enough. I wanted more money and vowed to make it even faster. I grew up with a solid work ethic. But the examples I saw for me equipped Satan with enough rifles, pistols, and machine guns to wage war on my mind and the uncorrupted work ethic that I should have inherited.

CHAPTER TWO

SALVATION

I was introduced to the Lord as a small boy by my father's mother, Fannie Mae. My grandmother loved the Lord with all of her heart. She dedicated over seventy years of her life, serving him and leaving examples for her family to forgive quickly and love unconditionally. I can still visualize my grandmother's bedroom, where she spent hours talking with God. Sometimes, she'd call me in to pray with her. I would fall asleep each time waiting for her to finish conversing with God; they would talk for hours. *"The Word of God tells us, the prayers of those who are right with God hold a lot of weight"* (JAMES 5:16). I'm positive Grandmother's prayers kept me protected, while I was too foolish to understand I was living a life that opposed God.

I never forgot the example that Grandmother set for me, the Sunday services, the prayers, or her humming hymns. Yet, living life on my terms seemed more appealing than living a life obedient to God. Living life on my terms almost cost me my life, like that night on Holly Road. It was a Friday night in the summer of July, when I busted open a flavored cigar to roll up a blunt. I decided to take my bike to drop off one of my deliveries—an ounce of cocaine—to a guy in Buckhead. I took a few back streets to get there. Most hustlers never traveled on main streets. After another shot of cognac and one more blunt, I decided to head back to the Westside. I came off of Marietta Street on my bike, flying down Bankhead.

I looked over and saw the State Troopers parked at the underpass, in front of the MARTA station. I shifted down. Overlook Atlanta was on my right. I knew I was high. I knew I had an ounce on me. I could've been paranoid, but I figured they would stop me for something, but I was determined not to go to jail that night. I blew through the traffic light. I automatically assumed they were going to chase me, and they did. I flew down Bankhead Highway, zipping in and out of lanes and dodging through cars. Bankhead was a winding road. I knew many people who lost their lives coming around one of those curbs.

I looked over my shoulder. The troopers were several cars back, but they wouldn't stop chasing me. I approached a fork in the road at Bankhead Highway and Hollywood Road. I figured I could stop by one of my homeboys' houses on Hollywood Road, park my bike, and take the troopers on foot, so I swerved right. At 120 mph, I lost control of my bike. It was almost like a force took over me and the bike. I felt like I was riding into the Twilight Zone. Something took over the motorcycle. I went up on the curb, my knee hit one of the telephone poles, I spun around, the bike fell, and coasted for about twenty-five feet with me still on it. There I was, lying in the middle of the road, in a bloody pair of shorts, a white T-shirt, and a pair of classic sneakers.

My first instinct was to get up and run. I realized I couldn't. I said to myself, *Gee, boy, you done messed up now.* My leg was open and twisted. I blew out my right kneecap. At that point, I tried to figure out a way to get rid of the drugs. I threw the bag that the cocaine was in; it spilled open beside me. When the troopers found me, one of them jumped out of the car and kicked me, saying, *"You thought you was gonna get away, didn't you?"* Thankfully, a lady pulled up yelling, *"Naw! Stop it! Y'all not about to do that! Get him some help!"* My accident was ten feet from the fire station, and a few of the firemen came out to help me.

Sirens blared as the ambulance pulled up. As he put me in the back of the ambulance, one of the EMTs said, *"I've been doing this for thirteen years man. You're really lucky. Three out of every five motorcycle accidents I show up to usually end in decapitations. I've had to find heads, arms, you name it. You just lost a kneecap. You're in good shape."* He left me to peel my kneecap off of the pole and put it on ice to preserve it. The death angel had an appointment with me that day. But I was snatched out of the grips of death.

The ambulance rushed me to Grady Memorial Hospital's trauma unit. I was losing a lot of blood. The nurses cut my clothes off of me, but I remembered I had twenty-six hundred dollars in my front pocket. I asked one of the nurses to take a few hundred for herself and put the rest up with my property. It would be no time before the police came in and started asking me questions. I didn't want them taking my money. She looked at me with the saddest look in her eyes and said, *"Mr. Washington, you're losing a lot of blood. You may have to get a blood transfusion. Money is the last thing you should probably worry about right now."* A team of doctors began to stabilize me. All of a sudden, they left me and ran to the man next door to me. I overheard one of the doctors saying, *"His girlfriend stabbed him thirteen times."* *"Stand clear!"* They shocked him with the AED, then again, a few more times. *"We're losing him!"* Moments later, I heard the sound of the flatline. His heart stopped beating. Out of nowhere, I gained a value for life that I didn't have thirty minutes before. I prayed, *Lord, I can't die now. I'm not ready. I'm not ready.*

I woke up the next morning with a catheter in, an external

fixation device holding my injured leg in the air, and my "good" leg shackled to the bed. The Lord honored my prayer. I was only twenty-three years old; I was terrified. I spent six months healing at Grady Memorial Hospital, after my bike accident. My doctor compared the condition of my leg to someone taking a twelve-gauge shotgun, pointing it at the center of my knee, and pulling the trigger. Doc gave me one of two options.

If I went with option "A," my leg would be amputated. If I went with "B," a special titanium rod, which would extend from my buttocks to my ankle, would be placed inside of my leg. I would live with a limp. I went with plan "B." Sadly, I chose to become something that I wasn't, because I had an audience that I had to impress. Everyone I knew in Florida still kept close tabs on me. They were all either anticipating my success or failure. What would they say about me now? I lay in the hospital every day wondering what people would say about me.

Like Jacob, my permanent limp is a reminder of my wrestle with God. God called Jacob; he was a part of the promise. God had something especially for him. But Jacob's name means "trickster." A dope dealer is also a trickster, who isn't his true genuine self. I was God's all along and didn't know that my identity rested in Him. My life was moving at the speed of my motorcycle that night. I became more and more unpredictable. My limp is a constant reminder of His grace and love for me. I wrestled for my will to be done in my life; He wrestled for His. He won.

Now that I think about it, the Lord gave me many chances to follow Him. I made good use of one of those chances on an early Sunday morning in February of 2002. I met a rev from the community, Reverend Samuels, who hired me to help with some repairs at his church. I started going to Sunday services at the church, but I would still live life on my terms Monday through Saturday. During one of his sermons that I barely listened to, I heard Reverend Samuels mention 2Pac.

Pac was my all-time favorite rapper. From that moment,

I started listening. After service, I walked to the altar, crying and confessing how much I needed Jesus. At that moment, I had a Damascus Road experience with Christ. The Lord met me at the altar, asking me why I would ever want to persecute Him. Me choosing to live how "Gee" wanted, regardless of the consequences that would settle on my life or anyone else's, was me persecuting Him. I couldn't give Him an answer; I could only cry. I accepted Christ as my sin-bearer that day. My life would be forever changed.

CHAPTER THREE

THE LORD IS MY SHEPHERD

I can recall October 31, 2002, like it was yesterday. It was judgment day for me at the Fulton County Superior Courthouse. I was on trial for trafficking cocaine and carrying a firearm. I was already considered a "convicted felon" for a few previous drug and gun charges I had. But, with the help of a very costly lawyer, I beat all of my other cases. Something felt different this time. My fate was in the hands of a majority white jury except for one black man. Before my arrest, indictment, or trial, I felt a tugging on my heart to change how I lived, and I did. But I wasn't confident the Lord would show up to court on my behalf.

One of the first scriptures I memorized was Psalm 23. That same prayer became the anchor of my soul in the courtroom that day. The psalmist's words, *"The Lord is my shepherd; I lack nothing,"* would replay over and over in my heart and mind for six hours straight. Judge John Bishop and the prosecuting attorney, Steven Holcomb, heard my case. We waited six hours for the jury to come back with a verdict. The night grew long; everyone's patience grew thin. Judge Bishop insisted the jury make a decision.

I was reminded of King David's words in verse four of PSALM 23, *"Even though I walk through the darkest valley I will fear no evil."* Initially, I didn't realize that my darkest valley wasn't what I faced in the courtroom. Up until that point, I lived eighteen years of my life in Sheol, outside of the protection of the one true Shepherd. Surely, my darkest moment wasn't coming to court to face my accusers. My court day could have easily not been a part of my story. I sold poison for eighteen years. The Father could've allowed me to reap death from the seeds of death I sowed. Rather than gaining a limp from my accident, I could've lost my life. I continued to pace the floor outside of the courtroom. *"I will fear no evil"* settled into my spirit.

My experience was faithful to the psalmist's words, *"Your rod and your staff, they comfort me."* We returned to the courtroom. The jury stood to their feet, and the spokesperson replied, *"We, the jury, find Mr. Washington guilty of trafficking cocaine."* BAM! Judge Bishop's gavel hit the sound block. His eyes met mine, and he said, *"Mr. Washington, you have been sentenced to twenty years in the Georgia State Penal System."* His words echoed throughout the courtroom, piercing my heart and traveling throughout my entire body. I was in shock; I couldn't process what he said. My attorney looked toward me and said, *"You'll only do forty months."* I thought to myself, I couldn't see what my lawyer saw.

My mother began to wail loudly. I turned around and motioned for her to be calm. I tried to hold it together. My family watched the bailiff take me out of the courthouse in handcuffs. My twenty-year sentence began that day. My release date was October 31, 2022. Some saw that circumstance as unfavorable, but I didn't. By the Spirit, Father God allowed something game-changing to happen on October 31, 2002. My situation wasn't just about another black man entering into our money-making machine called mass incarceration. God had a plan.

My first stop after sentencing was to diagnostics at Baldwin State Prison. From there, I transferred to Macon State Prison, where I completed the first twenty-two months of my sentence. I had my first conversation with God there, in 2002. I asked Him how my life spiraled completely out of control. I wasn't ready for His response.

Let's back up a little. Crack hit the eighties like a time bomb. It plagued almost every state in the country, causing added damage to poor communities. Crack, "the poor man's" version of cocaine, had—and still has—the ability to destroy lives. It would be completely "normal" for a crack addict to abandon or offer up their children, exchange sexual favors, steal, sell their prized possessions, or let the lights and water get disconnected for another hit.

Half of my friends in high school had parents who were using, selling, or doing a combination of both. One of my friends, Boss, asked me if I could "front" him and some of our other classmates a hundred dollars to buy a pack. He planned to buy some product to help his mother, Ruby-Ruth. They would work in shifts. When Ruby-Ruth would sell out of her product, Boss would pick up where she left off. Once he "flipped" the pack, he would give me back the money I loaned him, plus a little more on the top. This experience was the beginning of my life of crime. I had one of the best-paying jobs a teenager could have. I made sixteen dollars per hour plus gratuity, working as a line cook at a five-star hotel. Some days I made twenty dollars an hour. I had the money to loan them. Plus, with my mind already conditioned to get rich quick, Boss' offer didn't sound too bad.

Boss always made sure I got my hundred dollars back, plus an extra fifty. The money would come in as promised, and

I would loan him a few more dollars to up my return. Our business was starting to pick up, but we didn't have a good grip on the principles of hustling. Now, Ruby-Ruth knew the game. She put our community on the map, so to speak, for selling and using crack. We were "green." Hustlers can get hustled too. During our Drug Game 101 courses, led by Professor Ruby-Ruth, she would always find ways to get over on us. Boss got his product from one of the local kingpins, but he got it in a form we'd never seen before; it was powder. We brought it to Ruby-Ruth. She knew what to do with it. She cooked it up and transformed it into crack. The game changed for us.

Crack infiltrated our once suburban community. One of my uncles even fell victim to it. My Uncle would spend hours in the bathroom. We only had one bathroom in the house, which made his extended stays more obvious. When I finally had a chance to use it, I would walk in to see multiple crushed-up cans on the floor. I didn't get it. I couldn't get my young mind to stop wondering what Uncle was doing in the bathroom all of that time. Since word got out that I didn't mind "helping," another buddy asked me if I could invest in his new business venture too. Before you knew it, we had a shoebox full of ten- and twenty-dollar bills that totaled about eight hundred dollars. I made an honest living, only to invest that same money in destroying lives.

The enemy was in the midst. He encouraged me to take a few more "shortcuts" that would lead to permanent destruction in my life. I became too comfortable doing what I knew was wrong. My crew wanted to move on to bigger and better things. While still attending high school and working at the hotel on the weekends, my friends and I would travel to different colleges to party every weekend. We hung out at Bethune Cookman College with some of the Q Dawgs and tried to get our hands on a little weed to heighten our partying experience.

On one of those nights, we walked through a housing complex, where an older woman approached us. She asked if we had any base. That was quite a question to ask strangers. We all looked at each other dumbfounded and said, *"No."* But one of our boys replied, *"Oh yeah. I gotcha right here,"* while digging in his pants pocket. He sold her a gram of crack for fifteen dollars. Word got around. Before we knew it, we were visiting the projects every weekend, bringing drugs from Orlando to Daytona Beach. The money that we made fascinated us.

As I continued to walk around the prison yard, the picture of how I arrived at that place became quite clear. It was a mindset. The idea of making money—even if it was at the expense of others—took precedence. I didn't care who I sold to, or what measures I needed to take to be successful. I was willing to take the risk of selling drugs—and selling my life for that matter. I traded in everything the Lord blessed me with, in exchange for evil.

Some started hustling because they were raised in an environment that left them with few options. Selling drugs may have been a means to bring food in the house, pay the bills, or keep a roof over their family members' heads. Others may have accepted the lie that their value lies in what they have. They may want to take on the personas they see in music videos, not realizing that their favorite rappers, who glorify lives of crime, don't live according to their platinum-selling lyrics.

Some begin hustling as a result of fatherlessness. Most hustlers grow up in single-parent households, watching their mothers struggle to provide. Most young men have an innate and innocent desire to help their mothers. Unfortunately, the absence of a father leads a young man to accept responsibilities that are not his own. Studies show that adolescents who grow up in single-parent households are 17 percent more likely to get involved in criminal behavior (MARRIPEDIA. ORG).

At the age of nineteen, I approached, what I call, a fork in the road. In search of my identity, I chose the wrong path.

I wanted to make a name for myself. I wanted the money. I wanted to buy my mother a house and make up for some of what my father should have done for her. I didn't want to wait four years to finish college, then go after a career. I had a "now" mindset. I wanted people to identify with me as the one with the money and beautiful cars. My father never attended any of my events in my childhood, no sporting games, not my high school graduation, nothing. Because I wasn't affirmed as a child, by the one person I was seeking validation from, I lived life trying to prove my worth to everyone I encountered.

If we aren't careful, any of us could begin to measure our success solely based on what we have or don't have. I know this first-hand. My hustler's mentality contributed to me being materialistic. My designer clothes, hand-made Italian shoes, gold fronts, and old-school announced my arrival before I showed up to any scene. I wanted everyone to know I was winning. In my mind, I reached the top. Little did I know, it was the top of a two-foot ladder.

When the money begins to roll in, hustlers don't see the harm and damage they inflict on others. Along with materialism, greed develops. There will be an urge to possess as much as possible—cars, property, money, and women. These become gods to the hustler. The funny thing is enough never becomes enough. There will always be a need to secure another bag. A hustler's mentality doesn't allow him to cosider the damages and casualties caused by the game. There are fifth-generation crack-cocaine addicts and sellers who have single-handedly torn their families apart, chasing after a literal or figurative high.

God created us to live lives of joy and peace with Him and family. It's hard to find contentment in that which is real when we so willingly settle for a counterfeit version. In the book of Ecclesiastes, King Solomon said it would all be considered vanity. Everything that we acquire—especially out of selfish motives—would be left for someone else to enjoy after we leave this earth. *"Meaningless! Meaningless!, everything is meaningless!"* (ECCLESIASTES 12:8). The vain mindset of a hustler produces an emptiness. It robs us of our families, freedom, and—in many cases—our lives.

Satan entices hustlers with temporal possessions. He will ensure that his "end of the ride" moment will be a disastrous one. That is how much he hates us. The illusion of having great wealth in the illegal realm is just that. Jail and death seem to be the only two options for those who refuse to turn away from crime. I pray that you will begin to see the works of the enemy and the actions he takes to destroy us.

CHAPTER FOUR

"CINDY"

The mind of a hustler can play out in several ways. It's not limited to drugs. Cindy was a hustler too. She didn't start off selling crack, coke, pills, or weed. Stripping, also known as "dancing," was her "hustle." Cindy was a young, naive girl entering a world that would chew her up and spit her out. Cindy's dad left before she was born. He was married and had an affair with Cindy's mother. When he learned Cindy was on the way, he denied being her father and went back to his wife and children. Cindy had no examples of what a good man was. She was never affirmed by the first man who should have affirmed her. She accepted less than she deserved from every man who walked in and out of her life. Cindy had deep wounds, old wounds, that never healed.

She was dating a local dealer, Rico, who brought her to the strip club sometimes while he made a few discreet transactions. They had a son together, but shortly after their son was born, Rico got caught trafficking and ended up in prison. Cindy had dreams. She thought about becoming a teacher or a nurse or starting an after-school program for kids in the community. Cindy wasn't sure how, but she knew she wanted to help the next generation. She needed to take care of her son and make sure she kept her boyfriend's commissary up until he got out. One of her friends offered to get her a job working at Pink Flames.

A few of her friends were trying to become strippers or were already strippers trying to get out of the industry. She never looked down on them, but she promised herself she wouldn't be one of those losing her dignity for a new handbag and a pair of shoes. However, the thought of making fast money didn't sound too bad. She auditioned and got the job on the spot. Cindy went into the hustling game with a plan. She would dance for a little while, make some money for herself and her son, buy a car, get an apartment, and get back to working a nine to five. Unfortunately, her plans didn't go as planned.

Cindy was fresh meat—the hottest in the club. No one knew her or could say they "had" her. There was something still mysterious about her. Cindy would make a thousand dollars each night. The money she made from dancing was enough to take care of her and she took no time making it. Cindy got her first apartment in Atlantic Station, three months after working at Pink Flames. Not long after that, she put a deposit down on a new coupe. Her son was taken care of, she paid her bills, and Rico had enough money on his books to get him through the year.

When Rico called and asked how she was getting by, she told him she got a job at the hospital. She had to tell one lie to cover up another lie. Suddenly she had to battle with thoughts that didn't initially cross her mind. The idea of taking off her clothes for strangers disgusted her. She started drinking. Getting drunk before she got on stage temporarily eased the disappointment she felt.

Drinking led to private parties at hotels. Private parties at hotels led to popping pills.

Before she knew it, Cindy found herself drunk and high at parties when she was only supposed to be dancing. Her life spiraled out of control. She would have sex with strangers, most times not remembering what happened and sometimes not even knowing their names. She was in too deep. Cindy fell into prostitution. She would dance in the day and spend the night with two or three of her paying customers to make an extra five hundred dollars. Cindy was hustling and she used her body to do it.

She became addicted to the money and lifestyle. She thrived off of men paying her attention—even if it was negative attention. Cindy's value in the club started to depreciate quickly. While she was on stage, the guys used to come in swapping stories of where and how they had her. They would joke about her and say, *"Ol' girl went from 'top shelf' to 'bottom shelf' that quick. She's washed up; I'm not wasting my money on her."* Cindy didn't make nearly as much dancing as she did before. She spent the money she did make on getting high.

The calls from Rico didn't make it any better. He heard about her new profession. Rico would make sure she knew he thought she was trash, every chance he got. She knew that wasn't just Rico's opinion of her; that's what she felt about herself. Depression set in. To counteract the depression, Cindy started snorting coke and popping pills. She wanted to escape reality. Hustling overwhelmed Cindy. The streets got the best of her. She became strung out on crack-cocaine.

She lost custody of her son. One of her aunts became his primary caregiver. Cindy would spend the majority of her days walking up and down Bankhead Highway, now known as Donald Lee Hollowell Parkway, looking to exchange her body for enough money for her next hit. Rico got out of jail. He wanted nothing to do with Cindy. He was too embarrassed by her condition and by what his homeboys said about her. He went back to a life of crime with a new and improved (and younger) woman who took Cindy's place.

CHAPTER FIVE

"SEAN"

There's a misconception that "hustling" is limited to urbanized, gang-banging, gun-toting criminals—"street life." When we think of "selling something for gain," we usually associate the phrase with selling drugs or prostitution. However, hustling is any immoral act that brings gain. I know several guys who didn't sell crack or marijuana. They weren't "street dudes," yet they still acquired the mind of a hustler. Some of them went to college right after high school; others joined the military. They figured out a way to "beat the system," or so they thought, for their gain. White-collar criminals dabble in credit card theft, check fraud, identity theft, money laundering, cyber crimes, or bribery. They are no different from "boosters," professional shoplifters, who've mastered robbing high-end department stores to sell the products for half the price. Hustling comes in various forms.

Sean was nothing shy of a brainiac. He was one of the smartest at his school; he never made a grade less than an "A."

Sean grew up in a family of educators. His mother and a few of his aunts were teachers. Sean's father was a respected, long-standing assistant city administrator in Texas. Everyone knew Sean would go to college after high school, maybe start a few businesses, and live successfully. He was skilled in technology and earned a few scholarships that led to him attending college free of charge. Sean majored in business and accounting; he was good with numbers.

Shortly after graduating from college, Sean opened his first investment firm. He was a financial advisor for high-net-worth clients. Two years later, he opened his second. Sean's businesses were booming. However, he didn't see himself as Father God saw him; he had a poor sense of self-worth. His identity wasn't rooted and grounded in the Lord. Sean placed his value in his wealth, possessions, and status. Eight years after opening his second firm, Sean's world came tumbling down.

An audit revealed nearly a decade's worth of his shady business dealings. Sean was committing check fraud. He illegally printed checks using information from his clients' accounts, then funneled the checks into his offshore account. Sean would counterfeit thousand-dollar checks from his clients at a time. He figured they had more than enough not to notice. And seeing as he managed their money, Sean's clients trusted him. Once the investigation was over, the US federal government agents recovered nearly a million dollars that Sean stole from his clients over the years. He ended up with a hefty sentence in a Texas federal prison.

We live in a materialistic, commercialized, impulsive society. Many don't want to put in the necessary time to build credit—or creditability—and work hard for what they want. They're not willing to work their way to the top. The thoughts of developing that small business over the years, working toward the promotion, or completing college become daunting tasks. Media doesn't help the situation at all. We are constantly bombarded with the lifestyles of the rich and famous—the cars that cost more than houses, the mansions, the pictures of people wrapped in trendy Islamic fashion, camel riding in Dubai. These often grab our attention, forcing us into comparison mode.

All of a sudden, we begin noticing what we don't have, as opposed to being grateful for what we do have. We usually don't consider if those we're trying to emulate acquired what they have the honest way or by hustling. It doesn't take long for comparing to lead to compromise. We look for shortcuts to the top. We don't want to work hard, build retirement savings, or appreciate our journeys on the roads less traveled. We soon began to adopt a "by any means necessary" perspective to get what we want—now. We seldom think about getting to the root of those thought processes. We don't associate our hustlers' mindsets with the lack that we experienced during our childhoods, or our futile efforts to maintain the posh lifestyles that we may be accustomed to, or a poor sense of self-worth. Sooner than later, we lose all sight of our non-negotiables—those things we won't do for gain.

A dishonest Wall Street businessman is no different from a hustler standing on the corner selling crack. That businessman still has the same hustle mentality. His sense of ambition is distorted—regardless of if he wears a three-piece suit Monday through Friday. If he engages in fraudulent transactions, he's still a hustler. The gambler who cheats to win a professional sporting game bet and the dishonest prosecutor who breaks the rules to win convictions are both hustlers.

Hustling has become this glorified term we like to use to make ourselves sound productive. However, hustling is the total opposite of what God wants for us. Without being conscious or concerned with God's will for our lives, our treasures will lie in the here and now. We won't concern ourselves with building honorable legacies, nor the repercussions of hustling that affect our families. MATTHEW 6:24 reminds us that

"No one can serve two masters. Either you will hate the one and love the other, or you will be devoted to the one and despise the other. You cannot serve both God and money." Through that verse, God urges us to adopt an eternal perspective. If everything we value is here, on earth—if we believe this is our end game—we are in for a rude awakening. Yes, it's okay to be ambitious. But we have to be cautious of developing a "hustle-man" or "hustle-woman" outlook that isn't concerned with what we do, who we hurt, or what we forfeit to get what we want.

Hustling goes against the basic principles of how we're expected to interact with humanity. People are worth more than a printed piece of paper that doesn't hold much value. We break trust in so many relationships and devalue others when we hustle. When we lie, steal, and cheat, which are characteristics of hustling, we degrade both ourselves and others. Hustling is motivated by selfishness, masked by selflessness. Hustlers may use the excuse of making poor decisions to provide for their families, but that's not entirely true. Some of us like the idea of appearing powerful. When we feel insignificant, other people depending on us often makes us feel important. A college education or trade certification, leading to gainful employment, is what helps to take care of families.

When hustlers are caught in their transgressions and forced to pay their debts to society, they don't consider the burden that their incarceration places on their families. More than twenty million children in America live in fatherless homes. Studies show that fatherlessness is connected to poverty, increased high school dropout rates, teenage pregnancy, and crime. Hustlers take. Whether we hustle by selling drugs or stealing someone's identity, it's still taking. We're helping to destroy others' lives, as well as our own. Sean hustled with his intelligence.

CHAPTER SIX

AN ABEL OFFERING

In early 2005, after studying the book of Ecclesiastes, God healed me from materialism and released me from the bondage of selfishness. I stopped caring what other people thought of me—be it good or bad. I realized that many things in this life are vanity and leave us chasing the wind trying to obtain them. Outside of a relationship with God, I had nothing. I remember sitting at my desk in my cell, writing a letter to my brother Ken Carlos and sharing with him what God did for me.

I met Ken Carlos while visiting Atlanta for a weekend trip with my friend Braxton and a few others. Braxton would spend some time living in Orlando with his mother and Atlanta with his father. He graduated from Frederick Douglass High School in 1990 and convinced me to visit. My mother thought I was going to Atlanta to tour DeVry Institute of Technology. I was going to Atlanta to figure out the best routes to traffic cocaine from Orlando to Atlanta. A few of my friends from the neighborhood "hit a lick." They robbed some local hustlers for a quarter of a million in crack and told me about it. Since we already knew Braxton lived in Atlanta, we intended to go there to sell it.

Ken Carlos, knowing every road and back road in Atlanta, was our hood tour guide. I liked what I saw in Atlanta; it had potential. It wasn't long before I moved. Ken Carlos and I became close as brothers. Blood couldn't have made us closer. In the letter, I talked with Ken Carlos about us turning over new leaves once we were done paying our debts to society. At that time, I was serving my twenty-year sentence at Hancock State Prison and Ken Carlos was serving his time at Augusta State Prison.

I waited and waited for his response, but it never came. In late December of 2005, he returned. I remembered calling home and my mother telling me, *"Ken Carlos is home."* I immediately asked her to call him three-way. When he answered, I sternly asked, *"Bruh, why you ain't write me back?"* It was almost like he was rejecting the message that God shared with him through me. I soon realized that he wasn't interested in anything I shared with him in the letter.

Ken Carlos attempted to explain that he didn't reply because he knew he would be home in a few months and would speak to me then. But his response didn't sit well in my spirit. I could always tell when he wasn't shooting straight with me. He told me about a few people that came to visit him when he got home. They were the same people from our pasts, who were still selling and using drugs. It bothered me to know that he didn't feel a need to separate himself from what landed him in prison in the first place.

After we hung up, I went to speak with Brother Pete, Brother Micah, and Brother Alex, three men of God who served their time with me. We would all go to Bible study and fellowship together. Those brothers were some of the most impressive men I ever met. Pete had a master's in theology. Micah was the youngest of us all but zealous for the faith, like John the Beloved, and Alex, who was illiterate, learned to read by asking God to teach him.

Although prison consists of criminals who made poor decisions, it's still filled with human beings who have gifts, talents, and abilities. Pete was one of the first people to teach me about the Holy Spirit. He encouraged me to pray for the baptism of the Holy Spirit. Although I had read the Bible front to back, I never really understood any of it, until the Holy Spirit removed the scales from my eyes, like Pete said would happen.

I asked them to pray for Ken Carlos. If he didn't change, I knew it wouldn't be long before I heard he was back in prison, or worse. We began to intercede and pray for Ken Carlos's protection, for security, for employment, for God to meet his needs, so he wouldn't consider resorting to a life that he already overcame. I woke up the next morning with a story in my heart that I believe God placed there; it was the story of Cain and Abel. I read it a few times before, but I couldn't see how it was relevant to Ken Carlos and me.

The Lord then gave me another scripture from the Book of Proverbs, *"As a dog returns to his vomit, a fool returns to his folly"* (26:11). I shared what God gave me with Pete, Micah, and Alex. They believed Ken Carlos would return to his old mindset, based on the revelation I received. I was disappointed to hear that. I couldn't understand it. God blessed us both with another chance. We didn't have to spend the rest of our lives in prison—where we both deserved to be. We were both given an unmerited second chance. I wondered why he would want to go back and risk his freedom again. All of a sudden, GENESIS CHAPTER 4 began to make sense. I was "Abel" in the story. God received my offering.

A couple of years after Judge Bishop sentenced me to those

twenty years in prison, my attorney put a motion in for me to have a new trial. There I was, back in the Fulton County Court, in Judge Bishop's courtroom. To my amazement, Judge Bishop greeted me like he didn't sentence me to twenty years in prison just twenty-two months earlier. *"How are you doing, Mr. Washington?"* he asked. He went on to say, *"Mr. Washington, what's your release date?"* The only document I ever had throughout the process had a release date of October 31, 2022—twenty years from the time he sentenced me.

Once I reminded him of our last encounter, Judge Bishop looked over to the DA and said, *"What can we do for Mr. Washington?"* His attitude toward me was completely different; I was puzzled. The DA said, *"According to Georgia law our sentencing for one count of trafficking cocaine was sufficient."* If I were thoroughly aware of the legal consequences of my crimes, before I committed them, I probably wouldn't have been in this situation.

The penal system holds returning citizens who did not have, and still may not have, an understanding of laws and the consequences of breaking them. Educating oneself is vital, as ignorance is not a good enough excuse. I ran into too many returning citizens who did not—or could not—read. I saw countless young men, even teenagers, cop out to life sentences due to ignorance, illiteracy, and sparse representation. The cost of crime is just too high to pay.

Even though Judge Bishop's attitude toward me changed, I didn't feel like he was ready to move forward with the motion. Instead of playing the waiting game at Rice Street, I had my lawyer send me back to Macon State Prison. To get a little closer to Atlanta, where my family was, I put in a transfer to Hancock State Prison. Without me knowing it, my sentence got modified to ten years and I ended up only having to serve four.

God had a plan for me. My time at Hancock State Prison was up on March 7, 2006. I remember the long drive from Sparta, Georgia, back to Atlanta. I paroled to my mother's house, on the Westside. A friend that I met through the Angel Tree Prison Ministry, Sam August, was there to greet me. I asked my little brother, Hen, to drive me over to Ken Carlos's mother's house. I was excited to see him. To my surprise, he barely embraced me when we arrived.

He was high then and was regularly using cocaine. I'm sure he didn't want me to see him like that. It was just so confusing to me. In prison, we talked about living different lives and not going back to the old things the enemy always bamboozled us with—those things that robbed us of our purpose. As I stood there looking at him in confusion, it was almost as if I time-traveled back to GENESIS 4. After Cain killed Abel, God told Cain, *"Sin lies at the door. But, if you turn your heart towards me, I will accept you."* That was my prayer for Ken Carlos that he would turn his heart toward God.

CHAPTER SEVEN

NO LOOKING BACK ON

While I was paying my debt to society at Hancock, Sam and I would fellowship, through the prison ministry. He sent me Bibles and helped nurture my relationship with Christ. I remember asking Sam, *"When I come home, could I visit the church you've been going to?"* I wanted to be active in the community and used by God. Sam brought me to City of Refuge, in Atlanta, Georgia. I began volunteering. It was a great place to hang out.

I saw people sharing their time and giving their lives to those who were in need. On Wednesdays and Thursdays, a few of us from the church would serve hot meals on Jefferson Street, on James P. Brawley, and Northside Drive. As I went to hand a plate to one of the men in line, he said, *"Gee? That's you? You wit' the church now? Man, if you can change, anybody can change."* He grabbed his plate, shook his head in amazement, and walked away. That was the Lord letting me know that I was on the right track.

At that time, I was a person in need; I needed direction and guidance. I needed someone to believe in me. When I started sharing my testimony of how God delivered me from a life of darkness, the members of City of Refuge embraced and encouraged me. They would say, *"Greg, you're greater than your story. Your story is just something God gave you to inspire others as you move forward with your life."* My Christian journey outside of the gates began.

I tried to maintain communication with my brother, Ken Carlos. I confirmed that I had to live my life for Christ and that I couldn't return to the streets. Ken Carlos chose to return to life as we knew it. In 2009, he died of a heart attack—alone—in an Atlantic Station condo. Ken Carlos Lawson left behind several children. He was thirty-eight years old. I believed he had a lot more life to give; yet, that was his appointed time. His death was a massive blow to his loved ones. Ken Carlos was a decent person; he loved everyone. He would give anyone the shirt off of his back—literally. It was tragic for him to die the way he did.

In my sadness for my brother, I became encouraged. Ken Carlos's death charged me with a mission to expose the work of the enemy on the minds of young people, who become duped into believing making a living illegitimately really works. After not working for sixteen years, I was hired on with WIS International. The pay wasn't what I was used to, but I heard God calling me to a life of morality. I worked there for two years and earned the position of crew supervisor. Although I was grateful for my new role, I wanted a job that paid a little more. I knew I wasn't going back to my old ways, but I also didn't want any temptations.

I remember talking with my pastor, Ghetto Rev, and telling him I wanted to get a better job. My supervisor said he had to cut hours for two months. I could've easily got a pack and picked up where I left off before prison. But I knew that wasn't what God wanted for me. Rev reached out to his brother-in-law, John, who had close to twenty years invested with one company. John made a few calls and got me an interview. I got hired in the shipping and receiving department.

It was a job with benefits. It gave me a little more assurance that I was on the right track. I continued to volunteer and worship at City of Refuge—Mission Church. I was growing in a way that God wanted me to, even after suffering the loss of a brother. Ken Carlos and I were best friends, but I considered him my brother. Life became more meaningful as I continued living with the right mindset. I knew that I was a son of God who could live a productive life without selling drugs or undermining the system.

I stayed in contact with a few of the brothers I met while I was in prison. Alex Cruz was one of them. Before I left Hancock, I gave Alex the number to my mother's house and told him to call me when he got out. I didn't have much to offer him, but I did tell him I would try to help him if he needed anything. Rewind to 2006, while we were both in prison. God spoke to me about Alex.

He told me that Alex would have a family reunion. Alex spoke a lot about the condition of his family and the physical separation that they experienced for so long. Selling drugs was all he and his family knew. The hustler's mindset was a way of life for them. Several of Alex's family members spent significant time in jail. When one got released from prison, another would get arrested. When one got arrested, another would be released. They could never seem to be out of jail at the same time. Alex's family situation weighed on him for years. Alex's condition wasn't the only one God shared with me.

As I became more in tune with the Holy Spirit, Father God would reveal so much to me, including a revelation about one of my roomies' health. My roommate before him shipped to another prison, so I had space for Geech to move in. One of the codes of prison life was whoever was in a cell longest had seniority. They would set the tone, so to speak, for the room. I let Geech know all I did was work out and go to the chapel and Bible study.

From day one, I made it clear that I wasn't into selling or using drugs and I liked women. I never locked my lock boxes. I didn't care about any of my food or hygiene items that were in them. There was nothing in prison that was important enough to keep. I focused my mind on going home. So, I let him know he was welcome to have whatever he wanted. Our first night as roomies went well.

Geech believed he would be going home soon. He was excited about that. He got a letter from his sister, months before we became cellies. He gave it to me and asked me to read it. In the letter, Geech's sister let him know he was welcome to parole to her house. All Geech needed before his release from prison was an address to list on his paperwork, which he had the whole time. Because he could not read, he remained in jail longer than he needed to. I felt terrible about the entire situation.

I immediately spoke with one of the guys who was a leader in the education department, asking if Geech could enroll. The class was full, but I got the GED study books to help him on my own. While working with Geech, I was also studying one of Dr. Tony Evans' Spiritual Warfare Sermons. In one of the online sermons, Dr. Evans said, *"When you start studying this stuff, the Lord is going to reveal something to you."*

On the second night of Geech being in the room, I had a dream that someone was holding me down on my bunk. In the dream, I called out, *"Jesus! Jesus! Help me!"* I woke up feeling bound. All of a sudden, I heard the Holy Spirit say, *"Ask him if he's HIV positive. He will tell you the truth."* I was confused and nervous all at the same time. I turned on my worship music to clear my mind. Late that morning, I asked Geech if he had HIV. He replied, *"Yeah man. That's what they told me when I was at diagnostics."*

I think God was testing me to see if I would still treat Geech with the respect and dignity he deserved. The next morning, one of the inmates came to my room yelling, *"Greg! Something is wrong with your roommate. He keeps jumping in and out of the shower, butt naked, saying something is crawling on him."* When I got to the shower room, Geech was shaving his head and pubic hairs, yelling, *"They on me!"* Geech was bleeding from his head. I had never seen spiritual warfare in raw form like this. I was terrified. The guards ran in to get the situation under control. Geech moved to another facility. I never saw him again.

Alex was released in 2009 and called me for a temporary place to live. He was a native of Cuba. The United States didn't deport him back to Cuba but released him to me. We both found it funny for a prisoner to parole to another prisoner, but of course, the Lord can do whatever He wills. I had a condo in Marietta, with a spare bedroom. So, there we were, two parolees who loved the Lord. Alex was a great mechanic. I had a mechanic friend, who needed some extra help, so I introduced the two. Alex got hired on the spot.

I remember him coming home from work one day saying, *"Bruh, you won't believe it! All of my family is out. We having a reunion!"* I sat in silent awe, thinking about the goodness of God and how true to His word He is. I said to Alex, *"In a time when both you and I were isolated from the world, God used me to tell you that He would give you the desires of your heart."*

MIND OF MALIKA

Abandonment and instability high-jacked my childhood. I also wasn't a stranger to verbal, emotional, and sometimes physical abuse. I was a product of two teenage parents, one a native of Bronx, New York, and the other who migrated to the States from Havana, Cuba. Our family seemed to be destined for destruction before it even began. Both of my parents dropped out of high school, as most teenage parents do. Dad got a head start on a drug addiction that would last decades. Mom carried the weight of her childhood trauma that would eventually negatively impact her ability to maintain relationships, including ours.

Our family of three quickly split into a family of two— my mother and me. Since my mother was working on her GED and a couple of data entry courses, I lived with my grandmother in the Bronx—Murphy Projects to be exact. I can still remember my older cousins and me walking a cart full of

Grandma's empty beer cans over to Crespo's, on Tremont Ave. I was always excited when Grandma told us to cash the cans in and play her numbers. My cousin was usually embarrassed. But it never took long for his frown to turn into a smile when the half cents per can started adding up.

If we're not careful, we'll become what we say we won't. A month after my high school graduation, I found out I was pregnant with my first son. My plans for becoming a pediatrician quickly went out of the window. Survival mode kicked in. I couldn't think about the future; my priority became my son and our immediate needs. I tried to be the best nineteen-year-old mother I could be. But life led me to some hang-ups of my own. Fatherlessness affects young women just as much as it does young men. When our fathers don't affirm us, when they don't tell us we're unique or beautiful, we develop a yearning to receive that affirmation from somewhere—regardless of if the encouragements are attached to someone's ulterior motives.

Our sense of self-worth becomes so distorted that we'll accept mistreatment or words—made up of sweet empty nothings—from the first man that pays us some attention. In some weird way, that "man" replaces our MIA fathers. The fact that my mother and I didn't always see eye to eye didn't help my esteem either. Being told I was ugly, having my hair pulled out in scuffles, or being called bitches whenever we argued utterly distorted my perception of myself. I didn't yet understand who I was in the Lord. I wasn't aware of how much I meant to Him, regardless of anyone's attempts to strip me of my worth. I had support from family members, but nothing measured up to the idea of the fairytale family I had in my underdeveloped mind.

There I was again, pregnant with my second son, and still not married. My goal never was to be a "baby mama." I planned to wait until after marriage to have sex and welcome children into the world. I expected to be a wife. My mother did teach me the power of resiliency. I was a fighter, who didn't understand the concept of quitting. Grit carried me a long way and forced me to push to be the best provider I could be—even on the days I was too tired or discouraged to want to try.

In 2005, I wrote a heart-wrenching prayer to God titled, "These Things I Will Cast into the Hands of the Lord." When I finally realized that my life was nothing that I dreamed it would be, my emotions began to spiral out of control. I was a young mother, with two little boys. I wanted them to have the best, not the unstable childhood that I experienced. I'm sure I also wanted to make up for some of my mistakes. I figured working two to three jobs while juggling a few college courses would help me become the mother they deserved.

My letter included family healing and stability, emotional healing, and a few other requests that I could not provide for myself. I also prayed for a husband, but I gave the Lord specific instructions for him not to be a pastor. Even while living with one fought in the army of the Lord, and one fought out, I knew I didn't want the pressure that I thought came along with being a "first lady." I thought pastors' wives lived restricted, "under the microscope" lives. I sure didn't want to be the topic of discussion every time one of the sisters at the congregation opened their mouths.

There were two things I undoubtedly knew; I didn't want to be anyone's pastor wife, and I didn't want my boys to grow up in dysfunction, as I did. Even with two striking sons, I longed for a daughter. I added her to my list, as well. I'm sure that came from a place other than wanting to put frilly pink dresses on her. I wanted a do-over at that whole "mother and daughter" thing. I wanted to give my daughter what my mother wasn't able to share with me. I wanted to break the generational curse.

After praying over it, I folded the letter to God up and placed it in my Bible, trusting that He would honor my prayers. Two years later, I received a phone call from a stranger. *"Hello,"*

I said. *"Hello,"* the voice on the other end replied. *"Malika, you don't know me, but I am a friend of your father's, Santiago. He is being released from prison and would like to see you and meet his grandsons. Your family is having a family reunion."*

Of course, I was confused, angered, and excited all at the same time. My father went twenty years without contacting me. He didn't know if I was dead or alive. When I was about twenty-five, I got word that he was in the Georgia Department of Corrections system, and I looked him up. After confirming from his online mug shot that it was him, I drove a thousand miles from Connecticut to Georgia to visit him behind a glass partition. When he got out of jail, he still wasn't quite ready to be a father. His thirty-year crack addiction and unpredictable behavior wouldn't let him. The boys and I were planning a mother-and-sons trip that year; yet, I felt like they would want to meet their grandfather at least. So, off to Atlanta we went in August of 2007.

CHAPTER EIGHT

LOVE AT FIRST CONVERSATION

Years before Alex's family reunion, I prayed to God and asked Him for a wife. I said, *"Lord, I don't want to live a life of sexual immorality. You know I'm weak in that area. I don't have the self-control that I need to live a life of abstinence."* I begged and pleaded for the Lord to complete me—and not just for sexual purposes. I wanted to live as an upright man of integrity and not of degradation. I looked at faithfully married men with a desire to have the same.

The Lord holds out on information sometimes. He's a Master at not showing us His whole hand. Alex never told me he had a niece from New York who was living in Connecticut at the time. After the reunion, Alex invited a young woman up to see where he lived. The sound of heels clicking over the hardwood floors brought me out of my bedroom. I stood and started thinking to myself, *I know me and him spoke about not having no women up in here. She's beautiful, she looks half his age, and she got on pink heels. Bruh, what are you doing?*

Before I could get annoyed, Alex said, *"Greg, I want you to meet my niece, Malika." Niece?* Alex sure didn't say she'd be in town for the reunion. I quickly said hello and introduced myself. She responded, *"Hi, I'm Malika."*

Malika had only visited Georgia twice, once to visit her father in prison and then for the family reunion. She was staying at her father's house in Decatur, which was about forty or so minutes from where we were. She didn't know her way back to Decatur, so I offered to talk her back to her father's house over the phone. After navigating her back to her destination, we decided to stay on the phone. I told her about my entire life story. That forty-minute conversation turned into six hours.

We spoke about the mindset I fell into right after high school and me having so many opportunities at my fingertips but choosing the wrong path. Malika admitted that she wasn't living a life that was pleasing to God. I gently reminded her that if she repented and accepted Jesus back into her heart, He would take up residence there. God started coaching me in the middle of our conversation and reminded me of some talks He and I had. Several months before meeting Malika, I asked Him how I would be able to identify my wife. I didn't want to yoke myself with anyone that I wasn't supposed to. He said, *"Ask her if she would be willing to live a life abandoned to My Kingdom. She'll say yes without hesitation."*

Without feeling like I had much to lose, I proposed to her. I asked her what she thought about living a life dedicated to the Lord. She immediately replied, *"Okay."* By the end of the phone call, Malika made two significant decisions: one to follow Christ whole-heartedly and the second to marry me. She went back to Connecticut a few days later. We spoke every day, around the clock. Since I still owed Georgia time and couldn't leave the state, Malika would come to visit me.

Our morals went out the window. We partook in pleasures that made us feel disconnected from God and eventually detached from one another. According to the world's standards, our culture's way of life, if you meet someone, like them, and see yourself being with them, you're clear to have premarital sex. And so, we did, knowing that God expected us to do more than *"conform to the patterns of this world"* (ROMANS 12:12). Although we knew it was wrong, we continued.

Malika had earned a scholarship to Syracuse University. But several issues with her family and finding out that she was pregnant a month after her high school graduation delayed her opportunity to attend college. She wanted to be a nurse. We talked about her moving to Georgia for a fresh start. Attending nursing school in Atlanta and reuniting with her father sparked Malika's interest in relocating. She and her father didn't communicate for about twenty-two years before the reunion. He moved from New York to Atlanta when she was three years old. Malika didn't see her father for over two decades. I don't believe he intentionally set out to abandon her; nevertheless, he didn't father her. She located him a few times throughout her life, through online inmate locator systems. I know her heart longed to be closer to him, once they finally reconnected.

In the spring of 2008, Malika and the boys relocated to Atlanta. When she arrived, she found out that her father was still very much addicted to crack-cocaine. She was distraught and felt like she made the wrong decision to move. She was ready to return to Connecticut, but I suggested that she and the boys move in with me. I should have talked to Rev about it, but I decided I could figure the situation out myself. I moved Malika and the boys in; we were unmarried. We played house, but the house rested on a very shaky foundation. A few months later, Malika told me she was pregnant. I still didn't ask anyone for help.

We tried to figure it out on our own. Life was devastating for both of us. We were letting God down. We weren't living a life that was pleasing to Him. We fell victim to those mindsets that we could do things outside of the will of God and still be blessed. We continued to attend church, but our behavior was so convicting and weighed heavily on our relationship. We would argue daily. I'm sure we both thought us being together was a huge mistake. Side note, when we're wrestling with God about decisions we're making, we're not as bad off as we may feel. When living outside of His boundaries doesn't bother us, we should become afraid.

I called Rev to tell him about something the Lord laid on my heart. I felt led to share something with the youth of our church. At that time, we didn't have a youth pastor. Rev pretty much served as a youth pastor and senior pastor. Instead of him agreeing to me speaking to the youth, he said, *"You know, Greg, I can't let you do that. I got word that you and Malika are living together. That's not right, son. That's not what God wants for you two."* Malika and I had a meeting with Rev and shared that we were living in sin. We finally had the chance to air out our dirty laundry and stop hiding in shame.

Rev quickly helped us come up with a plan. I moved out of the house and into one of the spare bedrooms at the church. He arranged for Pastor Todd Jordan to lead Malika and me in premarital counseling. Man, I love Todd; he's a good man. But I knew his patience ran short with us two. He had to shake his head in frustration after some of those sessions. From a natural standpoint, we weren't ready to get married. Todd picked up on that very quickly. But God was doing something in the spirit realm; He was shaping us.

Malika and I began to understand that we were products of generational curses. "Generational curses" are considered negative traits or habits that have been passed down—in a family—from generation to generation. For example, Granddad was an alcoholic, Dad was an alcoholic, so now I've picked up the same behavior. Or Grandma fussed and screamed to get her point across, Mom fusses and shouts to get her point across, now I find myself unable to express my feelings without yelling and screaming.

But of course, God can use two broken people to break negative cycles in their families—even if they were affected by those cycles. Malika and I both had children from two separate partners and became a blended family. And yes, God brought that blended family together to live life on purpose. About six months into our premarital counseling, Rev agreed to marry us. The weight of sin was finally off of our shoulders. Although we still had some more work to do in our lives, I could see God moving.

MIND OF MALIKA

Premarital counseling was all done. Greg and I were set to get married by Rev—privately in his office. I did say in his office, right? Things were beginning to come together, but there was one thought I couldn't shake: I hurt God's feelings. In my seventh or early eighth month of pregnancy, I asked Father for a favor. I apologized again for my disobedience, but I was never really convinced He accepted my apology.

I grew up with a warped perception of God. I always felt like He was standing over me with a club, waiting to bop me on the head each time I did something wrong. I had no clue that once I sincerely apologized and repented—turning away from my poor behavior—He would forgive me. I've always pictured God as a tyrant, just waiting for me to do something wrong so He could punish me. As sad as it was, I feared that He would pay Greg and me back for our disobedience by harming our unborn child. I was way off. Sometimes, it takes time to unlearn the lies that we've learned.

Because of my perception of Him, the Lord knew I would need something tangible to calm my anxieties. On top of the overwhelming fear, I felt unworthy, unwanted, unaccepted, and unloved. I felt spiritually dead. That feeling of death immediately made me think about my Lord Jesus' death. I asked God to allow Laila to be born on Christ's Resurrection Day that year. I told God that I would know for a fact that He had forgiven me if He honored my request. Laila's Resurrection Day birth would be symbolic to my "dead" spirit reviving. I would then know that we were okay—that I made amends. I said the prayer once and never repeated it.

On March 22, 2009, Rev preached a sermon on restoration, rebuilding families, and a few other points that seem a little hazy now. But what I do remember so vividly were the words, *"And we're gonna have a wedding here today!"* *Huh? Whatchu talkin' bout Rev?* I looked around for a second couple that was planning to be married. All I could say in my mind was, *OH NO! NOT US! NOT HERE!* If you know Rev, you know how that story went. There I was, wobbling through the middle of the congregation eight months pregnant. I know, it was a sight for sore eyes. I know my Heavenly Daddy's eyes were wide open—happy to see His girl finally being obedient.

Greg moved back into the house that night. Things were finally getting on track. A month later, Easter Sunday rolled around. I was kind of on the edge of my seat in church, wondering if Father thought over my proposal. I felt a few cramps here and there, but nothing to make me think I would be going into labor. Sadness began to kick in a little. After service, Greg took our family—and Brother Carl, one of the brothers from church—out for lunch. After leaving Bay Breeze, we headed to Acworth Park.

Greg said Brother Carl and I walked off somewhere to pray, but I don't remember that. What I do remember was feeling like someone took a hammer to my uterus. I immediately yelled out. Quickly, I felt another internal blow to my lower body.

We all knew what time it was. Greg gathered up the children, helped us all in the car, then sped off to Wellstar Cobb Hospital. I was in labor. Laila made her debut so quickly. She almost made me miss my epidural. I wanted that epidural.

Within four and a half hours, I was staring at the most beautiful baby girl I ever saw in my life. Laila was healthy and was born on Jesus' Resurrection Day. The Lord God honored my prayer. Laila's birth wiped away every single lie I learned about God. Through her birth, He also affirmed His love for me and forgiveness of my disobedience. I am aware that my fresh start came at a considerable price. I am to live out the rest of my life in service, submission, and obedience to the will of God. How could I ever consider living any other way, after everything He did for me?

CHAPTER NINE

IS THAT YOU, LORD?

In spite of things going so right, something went wrong. The company where I worked was going out of business. I went to Rev and talked with him about what I learned. At that time, the first phase of Eden Village recently opened at City of Refuge. Rev suggested that I take on a position as security at the church. I did that for about three or four months and then another position opened. I became the warehouse manager, under Simon Grant's supervision. I ran the warehouse and oversaw the Compassion Atlanta program that we had operating at the time.

We would distribute food, clothing, and drinks to other ministries. While working at City of Refuge, I had a chance to spend time with a bunch of great men of God. One of those men was Gabe. I told Gabe my plans to re-enroll in college and gain some skills that would help me progress God's Kingdom. He was all for it and encouraged me to check out Atlanta Christian College (ACC), now known as Point University.

ACC had an adult access program that held classes at night. I was able to keep my full-time job in the day and attend evening classes. At that time, Malika was re-enrolled in college as well. She went back to pursuing a nursing degree but found herself overwhelmed and unsatisfied. The Holy Spirit spoke through me and I suggested that she go with me to Point University and pursue a degree in social work. She was always so willing to help everyone. Maybe the Lord wanted her to help others, just not as a nurse.

MIND OF MALIKA

I had just gotten back from another dreadful graveyard shift at the hospital. I hated the fact that I hated that job. I didn't want to be ungrateful. The extra income helped our family, but there were indeed days when I wondered if the Lord fell asleep on the job. I begged Him to remove me from that place. It wasn't the fact that I worked in the oncology unit; I enjoyed working there. I found fulfillment in caring for those who only had a few months to live. I wanted their last memories to be pleasant—even if they were in a hospital. I learned what spiritual warfare meant at the hospital. I faced opposition everywhere I turned—especially from those who confessed to loving God as I did. I didn't understand how that was even possible. Love God but treat the people who love God less than human? That was hard for me to digest.

I remember nights of praying against whatever force was working against me and some of my other co-workers. I remember evenings walking around the hospital unit, similar to the children of Israel walking around the walls of Jericho, praying those strongholds would come tumbling down. I remember periods of feeling resentment. I remember becoming frustrated with God. I didn't want to be there. I wondered why He wouldn't just give me another job and get me out of there. I knew He could. But of course, the Lord never slumbers; He sits high and looks low, seeing and empathizing with our frustrations. Not only that, He always provides "a ram in the bush." He arranged for me to have the sweetest conversations with patients who I knew didn't have too much life left in them. I led one of them, Constance, to Christ a month before she died. She was a twenty-three-year-old mother of two.

The house was quiet that morning, but my spirit was in turmoil. On the one hand, I wanted to become a nurse. I loved helping people. I was that way from childhood. Plus, I missed my chance to become a pediatrician and spent nearly six years chasing a nursing degree that always seemed to slip through my fingers. On the other hand, I felt like the Lord had something else in store for me. Like many of us, I wanted Him to bless my plan, rather than me be obedient to His.

As I sat on the couch feeling sorry for myself, I heard a voice say, *It's not nursing.* The voice wasn't my own, yet there was no one else in the house with me. The voice was audible, but in my mind at the same time. I immediately realized who was talking. I became upset with the Lord. I questioned Him, *What do You mean it's not nursing?* He didn't have any more time for my doubt or disobedience. He sternly replied, *It's. Not. Nursing.* I didn't ask Him anything else. I was too afraid of what He would say next.

The next day, I listened to the voice of God that came via a suggestion from Greg. I applied to Point University to begin my journey toward social work. Much to my surprise, Point accepted almost every single credit that I ever earned while pursuing a nursing degree. The Lord didn't allow those years of schooling to be years of uselessness—even if I was chasing a dream He never destined for me to pursue. Instead of nursing bodies, it was His will for me to nurse souls. So, there we were, a husband and wife, well beyond the traditional college age, walking the halls of Point University together. We watched God restore many years the *"locusts had eaten"* (JOEL 2:25). We graduated on the same date and shared another sweet victory.

CHAPTER TEN

LEVEL UP

About a year or so after Malika and I were married, I got a call from Ghetto Rev, asking me to come to his office. After we hung up the phone, I thought about what he asked for a long ten minutes. *People don't really like being called to Rev's office—especially if it's trouble. Is it trouble?* To my surprise, there wasn't any trouble brewing. Rev offered me the youth pastor position. I was in shock. I paused for a minute and thought about the affirmations I wrote while I was in prison.

I shipped to my main camp, which was Macon State Prison, on the same day my second daughter was born—March 21, 2003. I met Vince Randolph in the fall of 2003. Vince had already done about fifteen years at Macon State before I even got there. As I sat in the day room hardly understanding what I was reading in the Bible, Vince came up to me and said, *"You look like one of those guys who could make a collect call to his attorney. I want you to call your attorney and ask for three things: a copy of your indictment minutes, a copy of your complaint and af-*

fidavit—with signatures from the DA—and a book called Georgia Courtroom Rules and Procedures."

Staring at Vince with a frown, I said to myself, *Who is this old dude and why is he talking to me?* I didn't want to hear from Vince or anyone else. I was at a level-five prison, and I'd never been to prison before, just got a fresh twenty-year sentence and was extremely defensive. I was ready to put Vince on his back. He was saying stuff that I never heard before, so I stayed quiet and let him talk. Vince went on to say, *"You want to go home, don't you?"* I thought to myself, *Go home? What kind of question is that?* My parole date wasn't until October 31, 2022.

I gave him five seconds to get out of my face. Then Vince said, *"Take out a piece of paper and write down everything you want to happen in your life and write 'I am' in front of each affirmation."* Something told me to do exactly what he said. I began to write, *"I am in court this year and my case overturned; I am a man of God; I am at home with my wife and children."* On the back of the paper, I wrote, *"I will do great things in youth ministry."* I folded the paper up and placed it in my Bible. After that, I immediately called my lawyer. He accepted my collect call, just as Vince said. He also sent me everything Vince told me to ask him to send.

Five years had gone by before I looked at that paper filled with affirmations. But, on that morning, just a few hours before Rev called me into his office, I pulled that letter out of an old Bible that I used while I was in prison—five years prior. When I came out of the shock of what Rev offered me, I asked him to hold on a second. I went and grabbed the paper filled with affirmations and brought it back to his office. I started to cry. God showed me where He wanted to take my life. My only assignment was to be obedient to the "call."

Malika and I became youth pastors of the City of Refuge—Mission Church. We had no clue what we were doing. The experience was life-changing for us both. I planned to finish up at Point, attend seminary, and preach somewhere. But God had different plans. It's okay to prepare, as long as you leave room for God's alternations. While working with the youth, we met a young lady named Christina Johnson. Christina was a part of the youth ministry long before Malika or I started attending the church. For whatever reason, Christina wasn't attending church regularly.

God spoke so clearly to me. He told me that we should take Christina into our home just long enough to help her graduate from high school. At the time, Christina was sixteen years old but registered as an eighth-grade middle school student in the Atlanta Public School System. Susan, a friend of mine who was an advocate for children, supported Christina's move with us. Susan suggested that we quickly enroll Christina into the Cobb County School System, where our children attended school. She knew we would receive help for Christina there.

I let Malika know about Christina's situation and it broke her heart. Malika was very serious about young people receiving a quality education. She would quickly become frustrated at the sight of young people, young black people, skipping school or dropping out. She believed Dr. Martin Luther King Jr., Rosa Parks, John Lewis, and other Civil Rights activists fought too hard for equality, including for the desegregation of schools, for any one of our young people to quit school. Malika immediately wanted to help.

A part of me still wasn't convinced that Christina was supposed to live with us. I thought about the fact that we had a fixed income and five children of our own. Even preachers are guilty of doubting sometimes. God just kept saying, *"Do it. Be obedient."* Malika and I spoke with Rev about it and he backed us. The next day, Christina moved in and Malika took her to enroll in Floyd Middle School.

Malika remembered the school counselor looking at Christina's paperwork, looking up at Christina, asking her age, then saying, *"Oh no, this isn't right. Hold on a second."* The counselor left to make a call, came back to Malika and Christina, and said, *"You're welcome to go to the high school. Someone there will help you."* That day, Christina jumped a grade. She was a freshman in high school. Malika sent an email to Christina's high school counselor, explaining the situation.

Her counselor made sure that she only took the classes that she needed to graduate. And so, with her hard work, support from Christina's counselor, and Malika, who became her advocate, Christina skipped yet another grade and graduated on time—at eighteen years old. She got into a university, which was her first choice, in Tennessee. God took what would have taken her four years to complete and allowed her to complete it in two.

Our journey with the youth we encountered changed our lives. We realized, even more, that God placed us among young people to help restore hope and break generational curses that played out in their lives as a result of decisions others made well before their existence. Malika and I spent eight years in the youth ministry discipling young people, tutoring them, supporting them through high school, taking them on trips out of town each summer, helping them enroll into college, teaching them how to drive, preparing them for the workforce, mentoring them, and leading back-to-school drives and spiritual retreats.

Malika led Bible studies for the girls, mentored several of them through the National Guard Youth Challenge Academy Program, and taught them about womanhood and the importance of higher education. I spent time with the boys, modeling that manhood has nothing to do with how many women they could have premarital sex with or how many children they could father without the commitment of marriage. Aside from any spiritual impact we made on them, we were an example of an intact married family, which is often a rarity in the African American community. In many ways, we were surrogate parents to them all.

We worked with many youths in the 30314 community of Atlanta—the same neighborhood where I trafficked crack-cocaine. Father God gave me a second chance to make things right. We even had a few success stories like Sheldon, Kendra, Jeremiah, and Eva, our first high school graduates, and Shari, who was our first college graduate from the youth ministry. We became comfortable as youth pastors. But, as the saying goes, *"A comfort zone is a beautiful place, but nothing ever grows there."* We accomplished all that we could in the youth ministry. God was calling us to level up.

CHAPTER ELEVEN

PARDONED FOR A PURPOSE

When my life intersected with Rev's, we connected as a spiritual father and spiritual son. Rev asked me what my story was. I felt comfortable sharing it with him. I let him know about the years of selling drugs throughout the Westside of Atlanta. I didn't carry the dead weight of shame that I used to. I knew the experiences God allowed me to live through. I was a new creature. *"Anyone who belongs to Christ has become a new person. The old life is gone; a new life has begun"*(2 CORINTHIANS 5:17).

After our conversation, he immediately gave me a pardon. Rev's overlook, or willingness not to judge me based on what I told him, was symbolic to the forgiveness that I already received from my Heavenly Father. Rev's decision to overlook my past had much to do with him being in tune with the prophet Isaiah's words, *"Let the wicked forsake his way and the unrighteous man his thoughts; let him return to the Lord, that he may have compassion on him; and to our God, for he will abundantly pardon"* (ISAIAH 55:7).

Unfortunately, not everyone will embrace the new and improved you. Some will be skeptical. Some won't be interested in giving you another chance. If, or when, that happens, don't take it personally. At the beginning of 2017, I applied for a pardon on my trafficking charges through the State Board of Pardons and Paroles of Georgia. The Board denied me. The Board was not convinced that I was a rehabilitated man. I felt discouraged. The Lord quickly reminded me that He isn't like us, nor does He think like us. We judge one another based on what we see, based on what we've heard, or based on some false sense of street cred. But God looks at the heart. He knew that I genuinely accepted His offer to change.

When you learn who you are in the Lord, you'll begin to move with a different kind of confidence—knowing that no one, except for Him, has the final say. The Lord never gets "checkmated." He advised me to ask for character reference letters from Rev, Simon, Gabe, and other men from the church who could vouch for me. I reapplied with those letters. On May 10, 2017, I received an official pardon from the State Board of Pardons and Paroles of Georgia.

Let's take a more in-depth look at the Apostle Paul, as he wrote to the church in Rome. *"And we know that in all things God works for the good of those who love Him, who have been called according to His purpose. For those God foreknew He also pre-destined to be conformed to the image of His Son, that He might be the firstborn among many brothers and sisters. And those He predestined, He also called; those He called, He also justified; those He justified, He also glorified"* (ROMANS 8:28–30). Regardless of what crushing defeats you may have experienced, Father God can allow your mess to become your ministry. Pause for a second. Take a close inventory of your life. Do you have any past failures that the Lord wants to reconstruct in your personal story?

God never slumbers; He is always aware. He knew that

I would go to prison. He knew that He would release me before those twenty years were up. He knew that I would decide
to serve Him whole-heartedly. He also knew that my testimony would allow me to connect with, and understand, men
and women who have shared similar experiences. I don't believe God gives us pardons, or grace, to store up for ourselves.
I think He does it to encourage us to extend that same grace to
others. The Lord allowed me to receive an earthly pardon as a
tool for my next season.

CHAPTER TWELVE

RETURNING AND RESTORING

A year after receiving my pardon, Rev asked me to stop by his office so he could run something by me. He talked to me about transitioning out of youth ministry and offered me an opportunity to head up the reentry and reunification efforts at City of Refuge. I had about a week to make a decision and a month to make the transition if I accepted his offer. I was in shock. Youth ministry was what Malika and I knew. It's what we became comfortable doing.

After talking with Rev, I went home and told Malika what he and I discussed. I asked her to pray about my decision. The Lord spoke through her. She immediately asked, *"Pray about what? Isn't this what the Lord told you would happen? There's nothing to think about."* Sometimes we attempt to remain in our comfort zones, using the excuse of waiting for God's direction. Most times, He has already guided us and is waiting for us to be obedient to what He said. My hesitation about leaving youth ministry stemmed from disbelief. Sometimes we're amazed when He tells us something and it happens. Not because we don't have faith that He can do anything, but because we become overwhelmed by Him loving us enough to let us in on His plan.

Father revealed the importance of family to me and Malika years before we met one another. We both grew up in dysfunctional homes; we understood the damaging effects that unstable and unhealthy families could have on the generations to come. Out of our disappointments, Father God allowed us to develop a willingness to help repair and reunify families. Many didn't understand why we left youth ministry; everyone we knew associated youth ministry with Malika and me. It was almost as if being youth pastors were our identities. We now realize that season of our lives was our training ground.

In 2005, the Lord let me know that I would go back into the prisons—this time through the front doors. My poor decisions and past experiences aren't just stains on my garment. They are segues that allow me to connect with others who are trying to overcome what I overcame through Jesus Christ. I am charged with the responsibility of encouraging men to reclaim their roles of leadership. I am supposed to remind fathers that raising a family includes developing a firm foundation for that family—financially, emotionally, and spiritually. Because of my experiences, I also understand the support and the accountability, that men who are returning home need to live out their true identities. It's the same support that I received from City of Refuge when I returned home. That's what increased the likelihood of my success.

The process has to begin before returning citizens make it back home. They must face the remnants of anger, physical abuse, neglect, sexual abuse, fatherlessness, unforgiveness, shame, or any other injury that still haunts them. They must also address their unwillingness to incorporate structure into their lives or to check themselves when they make poor decisions. This process must begin before they exit through the metal bars. I stopped hesitating and accepted Rev's offer. And so there I was, within a month, off to The Ridge Project in Ohio, to become a certified TYRO facilitator.

TYRO—a Latin word meaning novice or apprentice, someone learning something new as a warrior—is a program designed to equip individuals with the life skills they need to be responsible parents and partners, better communicators, reliable employees, and positive role models. TYRO is a holistic, multi-faceted character-building program, designed to strengthen individuals and families. It was co-created by husband-and-wife team Ron and Cathy Tijerina. Ron and Cathy did fifteen years in an Ohio State Penitentiary together—Ron completed fifteen on the inside, while Cathy and their two sons did fifteen outside of the prison gates. From their experience, Ron and Cathy created TYRO, which altered the trajectory of their family—for the better. The program has been shared with hundreds of thousands, transforming families throughout the United States.

TYRO teaches men and women how to overcome destructive generational cycles that frequently tear families apart and keep individuals stuck in patterns of defeat. It also attacks the culture of entitlement and helps individuals become better men and women, leaders in their homes, communities, and workplaces. Programs like TYRO that address the issues concerning returning citizens are necessary. Not only do they tackle the breakdowns in how welcoming we are to returning citizens, but they also equip men and women coming home with the tools they need to thrive("TYRO 365," 2019). Returning citizens transitioning to their communities face pressures of unemployment, familial estrangement, homelessness, behavioral health concerns, addictions, debt, and unrealistic terms for repaying those debts—including child support. Without a support system, these pressures can cause returning citizens to make impulsive decisions—resulting in them re-adopting the hustler's mindset and recidivating.

When I arrived in Ohio for training, Ron and I shared our stories as we drove to a nearby prison to encourage some of the returning citizens. I immediately concluded that TYRO is an experience of men who are transformed in the mind, heart, and spirit. Ron often refers to men who completed the TYRO program as the "antidote." I don't think it was a coincidence that everything I felt during my incarceration was the same that Ron felt at the time Father birthed the antidote to the epidemic in him and Cathy's hearts. TYROs self-evaluate, and they determine what's important to them. TYROs come to terms with the consequences of their decisions. They also accept the fact that they've suffered some collateral damage along the way. Nevertheless, they don't allow their disappointments to dictate their futures. They work to better themselves and those they encounter.

When we start paying attention to the things that break God's heart, we'll see a side of Him that we never knew existed. He'll reveal certain truths to us. In less than a year of facilitating TYRO, I've come across many men who are trying to make wrong relationships right. I'm a witness to those men making efforts to work through some of the most challenging situations—most about their loved ones. If returning citizens throughout the world participated in a survey concerning their desires for family, I don't believe any of them would pass on having a healthy and thriving family. Those desires aren't limited to citizens presently in the process of returning home; we are all in a fight for our families and legacies.

In this season, the Lord is allowing me to help reunify and repair families. Believe it or not, it's become a norm for at least one family member, out of every family, to experience incarceration. Certain communities are hit harder—this is especially true of low-income communities. After so many years of imprisonment woven into the fabric of a family, the severity of the issue gets watered down. Returning citizens don't often realize that when we're incarcerated, everyone who loves us does time with us. Whether it's taking four-hour-long trips for a one-hour-long visit, paying costly phone bills filled with itemized collect calls, adding money to a monthly commissary account, not being completely honest with little ones about where Mom or Dad is, or paying for legal representation, we lock our families up with us. We also leave poor examples for the generations behind us. During my time at Hancock State Prison, I came across a grandfather, father, and son who were also incarcerated. Three generations of one family were disrupted.

We have to wake up. It doesn't matter if we're black, white, Hispanic, or other, or male or female. We cannot keep buying into the idea that crime will produce a payoff. It won't. Nothing is fascinating about prison. The pause button is pressed for returning citizens, while life moves on without them. Those who experience incarceration have two options for completing time. They'll either hustle their way through as if they were still on the outside or take time to evaluate how they got to prison in the first place and develop a self-improvement plan to move forward.

The choice not to recidivate also has much to do with one's mindset. I wasn't in denial of being a convicted felon at the time of my release, but I made a choice not to adopt a victim mentality. I didn't blame anyone for my situation. I accepted responsibility for my decisions and thanked God for His mercy —He didn't allow me to get hit with the time I truly deserved. When I left Hancock State Prison, I knew I owed it to myself, and the others who were waiting to come home, not to go back to prison. I focused on life after prison—the present.

When I mentor guys coming home, I stress the importance of them developing a pre-release plan. The light-bulb has to come on for them while they're still in a controlled environment. Time spent in prison is time for returning citizens to decide what they are not willing to do, to protect their freedom. Time spent incarcerated is time to come up with a non-negotiables list. This is a process that must be completed before the gates open. When I came up with my list, I vowed not to compromise my faith for anyone. Living for God wasn't a jail-house religion that I picked up to pass the time in prison; I was serious about it.

I accepted Christ before I went to prison but couldn't figure out the process. I now understand that the process is the process of "being saved." For those of us who have accepted Christ, we will continue to remain on the course of being saved as long as we live on this side of life. After five years of living out my Christian journey behind the walls, I knew I had to come out and continue the process—regardless of any distractions that attempted to keep me in bondage to the mindset of a hustler. When I fell short, I knew I would have to get back up and get back on the journey. I already had a plan to continue reading my Bible, praying, and fasting—all those things that changed me into a man of integrity.

I came home and continued the journey the Lord had me on while I was incarcerated. I'd be lying if I said it was easy; it wasn't. But I knew it was the right thing to do. I wanted to be obedient. The Lord blesses our obedience. I never asked for the youth pastor position; the Lord spoke it. I never asked to go back into the prison through the front gate; the Lord spoke it. When He says something, He means it. We must put ourselves in a position to first hear Him, then obey His word. We must get connected with the Navigator of our souls.

Sure, I know everyone won't believe in the saving power of Jesus Christ. But without that relationship, that anchor, we'll chase the wind and come up empty-handed. In the words of French philosopher Pierre Teilhard de Chardin, *"We are not human beings having a spiritual experience. We are spiritual beings having a human experience."* Take an in-depth look inward. Search your soul. Is there anything in your life that you need to address?

I am reminded of a sermon Dr. Tony Evans preached a while back. He mentioned the dash between the years of our birth and the years of our demise. He urged us to work on the dash—what we do with the time we have on earth. What will people say you stood for when you're long gone? What made you unique? What did you do for your family? What did you do for those who were in need? How did you impact the world? What were you passionate about? As you work to do away with the mind of a hustler and become a man or woman worth following, consider your dash of life.

ACKNOWLEDGMENTS

First, I would like to thank Father God and my Lord and Savior, Jesus Christ. Out of obedience to what the Holy Spirit spoke in 2005 about this book, *Mind of a Hustler,* the glory and first fruits of thanksgiving must be given to Him.

There are many to thank for believing in me, Greg Washington. I am grateful for my journey of becoming a husband, father, son, pastor, friend, and mentor. Hopefully, my service has been honorable to those I love and care for. To my wife, Malika Washington, thank you for falling in love with my story from the first day we met. As a result of you saying "yes," our stories collided, revealing itself as the Father's plan and not our own. Being a blended family has had its challenges, but thank you for believing in what the Father spoke over us some years ago. We fought to break generational curses within our families for generations to come. Love is the umbilical cord that sustains and nurtures our union.

I am thankful for the City of Refuge—Mission Church. I have been blessed to grow as a professional leader and Kingdom-minded faithful follower of Christ for the last fourteen years. I have the pleasure of working with some amazing people who are passionate about making others better than them. City of Refuge taught me that one comes to the City of Refuge to become a place of refuge for others. The "call" is for all who visit—whether they are donors, volunteers, staff, or recipients of services—we are all "called."

There were several who challenged me to dream big about the book. Special thanks to Cym Lowell for creating a foundation for the project. My dear friend and ministry partner, Jeff Orsenigo, and our Building Your Legacy family supported me throughout the process. Thank you to the Atlanta Resource Foundation, and many others, for your financial contributions. *Mind of a Hustler* would not have been possible without the creativity and direction of Hein van der Heijden, Atlanta's Best Graphic Designer and Illustrator for 2019. Lastly, I would like to thank BookLogix and all of those who support *Mind of a Hustler*.

GREG & MALIKA

Greg and Malika Washington are partners in life and ministry. The two vowed that their marriage would be a game-changer. Greg and Malika intentionally work together to break generational cycles in their family lineages, as well as the many families they encounter. Greg's passion for the word of God created a foundation for his reverendship. Malika's desire to "nurse" souls and equip families with the tools they need to thrive encouraged her to pursue a career in the field of social work. Greg and Malika use their God-given talents, strengths, and abilities to impact lives all around them. Together, they have five children—three daughters and two sons.